Literacy for Li

Reception - Term 3

Introduction

This book is one of a series. It provides a complete structured resource for teaching the phonics, spelling, vocabulary and grammatical work required by the National Curriculum for teaching English, 2014.

It includes:

- Word lists of spelling patterns
- Phonic matching exercises
- Comprehension and cloze procedure activities
- Dictation and sound differentiation units

One sound builds upon and reinforces the sounds preceding it. The consonant blends and clusters have been organised in logical sound patterns. Each unit follows the pattern set out by the Dept. for Education and supports the teaching of phonics.

If you purchased the original series there have been many changes made to the order in which sounds are taught and the level of work expected each term. So the text has been re-written and re-ordered to reflect the challenges and requirements of the 2014 curriculum.

We hope you will enjoy using this work and welcome your feedback and comments.

Kath Paterson
Egon Publishers Ltd

Suggestions for using this book

Word Lists

- Learn, copy then cover, write then check
- Can be given as a homework sheet

Sound Matching Activity

- Matching word with picture improves comprehension
- Includes colour word recognition
- Can be used as a class activity

LITERACY FOR LIFE
Consonant Blends & Sound Matching
Reception - Term 3

Extension Activities

- Follow up work
- Includes cloze procedure exercises for context and comprehension

Sound Differentiation Exercises

- Highlights a particular sound
- Contains comprehension activities
- Can be used as dictation exercises
- Shared or paired reading passages
- Activities to extend writing skills

by Kathleen Paterson

Consonant Blends
and Sound Matching

Reception - Term 3
2014 English Curriculum

Egon Publishers Ltd

Literacy for Life: Consonant Blends and Sound Matching

Reception - Term 3

Kathleen Paterson

ISBN: 978 1907656 06 4

Published in UK: 2014

Egon Publishers Ltd
618 Leeds Road
Outwood
Wakefield   WF1 2LT
Tel/FAX: 01924 871697
www.egon.co.uk

Egon Publishers Ltd (Company No: 1336483)

Literacy for Life, Reception - Term 3

Contents

Literacy for Life - Reception

Contents of Terms 1 and 2

Name_ _ _ _ _ _ _ _ _ _ _ _ _ _ _ _ Day _ _ _ _ _ _ _ _

learn it	copy then cover	write then check
brush		
brick		
crab		
crib		
drip		

Fold over

1

Name_ _ _ _ _ _ _ _ _ _ _ _ _ _ Day _ _ _ _ _ _ _ _

Match the words and pictures. Colour each word box a different colour and use the same crayon to join each word to the correct picture.

| brush |

| brick |

| crab |

| crib |
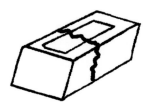

| drip |

Name _ _ _ _ _ _ _ _ _ _ _ _ _ Day _ _ _ _ _ _ _ _ _

Copy these words.

brush	brick	crab	crib	drip
_____	_____	_____	_____	_____

Choose the right word for each space below.

1. The _ _ _ _ can nip.

2. A doll is in the _ _ _ _ .

3. The _ _ _ _ _ has a crack in it.

4. _ _ _ _ is wet.

5. This is a _ _ _ _ _ .

3

Name _ _ _ _ _ _ _ _ _ _ _ _ _ _ _ Day _ _ _ _ _ _ _ _ _

learn it	copy then cover	write then check
grin		
frog		
from		
pram		
tram		

Fold over

Name_ _ _ _ _ _ _ _ _ _ _ _ _ _ _ _ _ Day _ _ _ _ _ _ _ _ _

Match the words and pictures. Colour each word box a different colour and use the same crayon to join each word to the correct picture.

grin

tram

pram

frog

from

Name _ _ _ _ _ _ _ _ _ _ _ _ _ _ Day _ _ _ _ _ _ _ _ _ _

Copy these words.

grin	frog	from	tram	pram

Choose the right word for each space below.

1. Go away _ _ _ _ here.

2. The man has a glad _ _ _ _ .

3. The _ _ _ _ is wet.

4. Is a doll in this _ _ _ _ ?

5. A man got on the _ _ _ _ .

Name _ _ _ _ _ _ _ _ _ _ _ _ _ _ Day _ _ _ _ _ _ _ _ _

Circle or highlight the correct word.

 frog   crib   crab   drip

 from   frog   pram   tram

 drip   grin   brick   brush

 tram   pram   grin   crab

 from   drip   tram   pram

 brick   crab   drip   grin

Name _ _ _ _ _ _ _ _ _ _ _ _ _ _ Day _ _ _ _ _ _ _ _ _ _

Underline or highlight the words which which begin with 'br', 'cr', 'dr', 'fr', 'gr', 'pr' and 'tr'.

The crab and the frog get on a brick.

The girl can go on a trip in a tram, with a doll in a pram.

Name_ _ _ _ _ _ _ _ _ _ _ _ _ _ Day _ _ _ _ _ _ _ _

learn it	copy then cover	write then check
black		
blot		
clock		
clap		
glad		

Name_ _ _ _ _ _ _ _ _ _ _ _ _ _ _ _ Day _ _ _ _ _ _ _ _ _

Match the words and pictures. Colour each word box a different colour and use the same crayon to join each word to the correct picture.

| black |

| blot |

| clock |

| clap |

| glad |

Name _ _ _ _ _ _ _ _ _ _ _ _ _ Day _ _ _ _ _ _ _ _ _

Copy these words.

black	blot	clock	clap	flag

Choose the right word for each space below.

1. The _ _ _ _ is _ _ _ _ _ .

2.  The _ _ _ _ _ rang at 6:23.

3. He did three _ _ _ _ s.

4. The _ _ _ _ flaps in the wind.

Name_ _ _ _ _ _ _ _ _ _ _ _ _ _ _ _ _ _ Day _ _ _ _ _ _ _ _ _

learn it	copy then cover	write then check
glass		
flag		
play		
plum		
slug		

Fold over

Name _ _ _ _ _ _ _ _ _ _ _ _ Day _ _ _ _ _ _ _ _ _

Match the words and pictures. Colour each word box a different colour and use the same crayon to join each word to the correct picture.

glass

flag

play

plum

slug

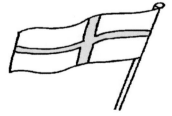

Name_ _ _ _ _ _ _ _ _ _ _ _ _ _ _ _ _ Day _ _ _ _ _ _ _ _

Copy these words.

flag	glass	play	plum	slug

Choose the right word for each space below.

1. The _ _ _ _ is on the _ _ _ _ s.

2. Drip _ _ _ _ s hoop-la.

3. Do not drop the _ _ _ _ _ _ .

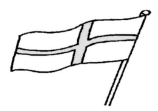

4. This is a _ _ _ _ .

Name _ _ _ _ _ _ _ _ _ _ _ _ _ Day _ _ _ _ _ _ _ _ _ _

Circle or highlight the correct word.

   black   clock   clap   glad

   plum   play   slug   black

   clap   black   clock   blot

   slug   plum   glad   glass

   flag   slug   play   plum

   black   blot   plum   slug

Name _ _ _ _ _ _ _ _ _ _ _ _ _ _ Day _ _ _ _ _ _ _ _ _

Underline or highlight the words which begin with 'bl', 'cl', 'fl', 'gl', 'pl' and 'sl'.

The clock struck six. The man had a shock. His glass fell with a crash.

He got a black blot on his top.

Name_ _ _ _ _ _ _ _ _ _ _ _ _ _ Day _ _ _ _ _ _ _ _ _

learn it	copy then cover	write then check
dwell		
dwarf		
swim		
swing		
swan		

Fold over

Name_ _ _ _ _ _ _ _ _ _ _ _ _ _ _ Day _ _ _ _ _ _ _ _ _

Match the words and pictures. Colour each word box a different colour and use the same crayon to join each word to the correct picture.

dwell

dwarf

swing

swim

swan

Name _ _ _ _ _ _ _ _ _ _ _ _ _ _ _ Day _ _ _ _ _ _ _ _ _ _

Copy these words.

dwell	dwarf	swing	swim	swan

Choose the right word for each space below.

1. The _ _ _ _ _ _ will fix the _ _ _ _ _ _ .

2.  She can _ _ _ _ .

3. The _ _ _ _ can swim too.

4. Pod _ _ _ _ _ s here.

19

Name_ _ _ _ _ _ _ _ _ _ _ _ _ _ _ _ _ _ Day _ _ _ _ _ _ _ _ _

learn it	copy then cover	write then check
twist		
twig		
twin		
twelve		
twenty		

Fold over

Name_ _ _ _ _ _ _ _ _ _ _ _ _ _ _ _ _ Day _ _ _ _ _ _ _ _

Match the words and pictures. Colour each word box a different colour and use the same crayon to join each word to the correct picture.

| twist |

| twig |

| twin |

| twelve |

| twenty |

Name _ _ _ _ _ _ _ _ _ _ _ _ _ _ _ Day _ _ _ _ _ _ _ _ _ _

Copy these words.

twist	twig	twin	twelve	twenty

Choose the right word for each space below.

1. The _ _ _ _ s can hop and skip.

2. The _ _ _ _ fell onto the grass.

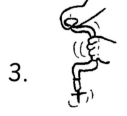

3. He had to _ _ _ _ _ the drill.

4. _ _ _ _ _ _ _ eggs in a nest.

5. _ _ _ _ _ _ _ mugs in a box.

Name _ _ _ _ _ _ _ _ _ _ _ _ _ _ Day _ _ _ _ _ _ _ _ _ _

Circle or highlight the correct word.

   dwell   dwarf   twelve   swan

   twist   swan   swim   swing

   twig   swing   swan   swim

   twig   twist   twin   twenty

   twelve   twenty   twist   twin

   swim   swan   swing   twist

Name _ _ _ _ _ _ _ _ _ _ _ _ _ _ Day _ _ _ _ _ _ _ _ _ _

Underline or highlight the words which begin with 'dw', 'sw' and 'tw'.

The two swans swim on the pond as

Drip has a swing and the twins hop and

skip.

Jack the dwarf can twist his drill

twelve times.

Name_ _ _ _ _ _ _ _ _ _ _ _ _ _ _ _ Day _ _ _ _ _ _ _ _ _ _

learn it	copy then cover	write then check
Scot		
skull		
skip		
snack		
snap		

Fold over

Name_ _ _ _ _ _ _ _ _ _ _ _ _ _ Day _ _ _ _ _ _ _ _ _

Match the words and pictures. Colour each word box a different colour and use the same crayon to join each word to the correct picture.

Scot

skull

skip

snack

snap

26

Name _ _ _ _ _ _ _ _ _ _ _ _ _ _   Day _ _ _ _ _ _ _ _ _ _

Copy these words.

Scot	skull	skip	snack	snap

Choose the right word for each space below.

1. This _ _ _ _ has a kilt on.

2. Blip _ _ _ _ s in the sun.

3. This is a _ _ _ _ _.

4. _ _ _ _ this stick.

5. The man has a _ _ _ _ _.

Name_ _ _ _ _ _ _ _ _ _ _ _ _ _ _ _ _ _ Day _ _ _ _ _ _ _ _ _ _

learn it	copy then cover	write then check
spot		
spin		
stick		
small		
smell		

Fold over

Name_ _ _ _ _ _ _ _ _ _ _ _ _ _ _ _ _ _ Day _ _ _ _ _ _ _ _ _

Match the words and pictures. Colour each word box a different colour and use the same crayon to join each word to the correct picture.

spot

spin

stick

small

smell

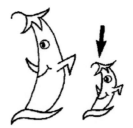

Name _ _ _ _ _ _ _ _ _ _ _ _ _ _   Day _ _ _ _ _ _ _ _ _

Copy these words.

spot	spin	stick	small	smell

Choose the right word for each space below.

1. Is this Pod big or _ _ _ _ _ ?

2. The man has a bad _ _ _ _.

3. The top _ _ _ _ s.

4. He can _ _ _ _ _ his lunch.

5. Snap this _ _ _ _ _.

30

Name _ _ _ _ _ _ _ _ _ _ _ _ _ _ Day _ _ _ _ _ _ _ _ _

Circle or highlight the correct word.

   Scot   skip   skull   spin

   small   skull   skip   Scot

   snap   spin   spot   stick

   small   smell   snap   skull

   snack   spot   spin   smell

   skull   small   stick   spot

Name _ _ _ _ _ _ _ _ _ _ _ _ _ Day _ _ _ _ _ _ _ _ _

Underline or highlight the words that begin with 'sc', 'sk', 'sm', 'sn', 'sp', and 'st'.

The Scot went for a spin in his small van.

He had a stop for a snack in a picnic

spot.

He put his trash in a bag and shut it

with a snap.

Name_ _ _ _ _ _ _ _ _ _ _ _ _ _ _ _ Day _ _ _ _ _ _ _ _ _ _

learn it	copy then cover	write then check
scrub		
scrap		
sprig		
spring		
splash		

Fold over

Name_ _ _ _ _ _ _ _ _ _ _ _ _ _ _ Day _ _ _ _ _ _ _ _ _

**Match the words and pictures.   Colour each word box
a different colour and use the same crayon to join
each word to the correct picture.**

scrub

scrap

sprig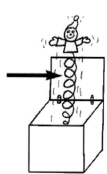

spring

splash

Name _ _ _ _ _ _ _ _ _ _ _ _ _ _ _ Day _ _ _ _ _ _ _ _ _

Copy these words.

scrub	scrap	sprig	spring	splash
_____	_____	_____	_____	_____

Choose the right word for each space below.

1. Pot will _ _ _ _ _ _ as he _ _ _ _ _ _ s.

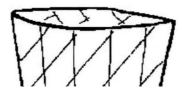

2. He took the _ _ _ _ _ to the tip.

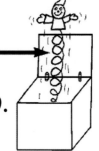

3. The Jack-in-the-box _ _ _ _ _ _ s up.

4. This is a small _ _ _ _ _ _ .

Name_ _ _ _ _ _ _ _ _ _ _ _ _ _ _ _ Day _ _ _ _ _ _ _ _ _

learn it	copy then cover	write then check
squash		
three		
thrush		
string		
shrub		

Fold over

Name_ _ _ _ _ _ _ _ _ _ _ _ _ _ _ Day _ _ _ _ _ _ _ _ _

Match the words and pictures. Colour each word box a different colour and use the same crayon to join each word to the correct picture.

| squash |

| three |

| thrush |

| string |

| shrub |

Name _ _ _ _ _ _ _ _ _ _ _ _ _ Day _ _ _ _ _ _ _ _ _

Copy these words.

squash	three	thrush	string	shrub
_____	_____	_____	_____	_____

Choose the right word for each space below.

1. A dog hid in the _ _ _ _ _ s.

2. She can _ _ _ _ _ _ _ a tomato.

3. This is a _ _ _ _ _ _ .

4. I am _ _ _ _ _ _ .

5. Here is a _ _ _ _ _ _ _ of beads.

Name _ _ _ _ _ _ _ _ _ _ _ _ _ Day _ _ _ _ _ _ _ _ _

Circle or highlight the correct word.

 sprig　splash　scrap　scrub

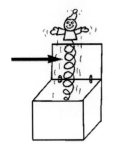 squash　scrap　spring　sprig

 splash　squash　spring　string

 three　thrust　thrush　shrub

three　thrust　thrash　three　splash

thrust　thrash　three　splash

 spring　string　shrub　squash

Name _ _ _ _ _ _ _ _ _ _ _ _ _ _ Day _ _ _ _ _ _ _ _ _

Underline or highlight the words which begin with 'scr', 'spr', 'spl', 'squ', 'thr', 'str' and 'shr'.

In Spring the thrush will splash in a bath. He will get twigs and sprigs to make a nest.

Pot is sad as he scrubs and splashes and gets wet.

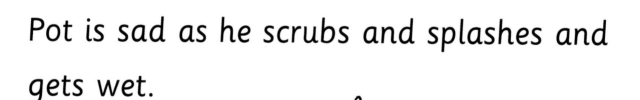

Name_ _ _ _ _ _ _ _ _ _ _ _ _ _ _ Day _ _ _ _ _ _ _ _ _

learn it	copy then cover	write then check
cold		
old		
milk		
help		
salt		

Fold over

Name_ _ _ _ _ _ _ _ _ _ _ _ _ _ _ _ _ Day _ _ _ _ _ _ _ _ _

Match the words and pictures. Colour each word box a different colour and use the same crayon to join each word to the correct picture.

cold

old

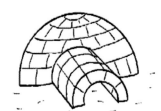

milk

help

salt

Name _ _ _ _ _ _ _ _ _ _ _ _ _ _ _ Day _ _ _ _ _ _ _ _ _ _

Copy these words.

cold	old	milk	help	salt
_____	_____	_____	_____	_____

Choose the right word for each space below.

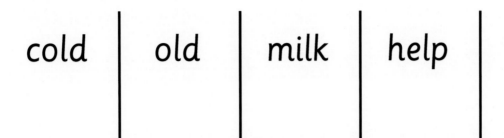

1. This igloo is _ _ _ _ .

2. He had a cup of _ _ _ _ .

3. We must _ _ _ _ him.

4. I put _ _ _ _ on my chips.

5. This teddy is _ _ _ .

Name_ Day _ _ _ _ _ _ _ _ _ _ _

learn it	copy then cover	write then check
melt		
quilt		
shelf		
half		
filth		

Fold over

44

Name_ _ _ _ _ _ _ _ _ _ _ _ _ _ _ Day _ _ _ _ _ _ _ _

**Match the words and pictures. Colour each word box
a different colour and use the same crayon to join
each word to the correct picture.**

melt

quilt

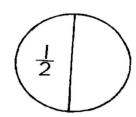

shelf

half

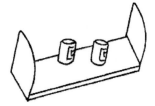

filth

Name _ _ _ _ _ _ _ _ _ _ _ _ Day _ _ _ _ _ _ _ _ _

Copy these words.

melt	quilt	shelf	half	filth

Choose the right word for each space below.

1. The _ _ _ _ _ is on the bed.

2. 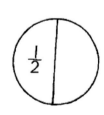 The sun will _ _ _ _ him.

3. _ _ _ _ the _ _ _ _ _ is in the bin.

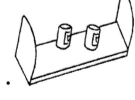

4. I put the cans on the _ _ _ _ _ .

46

Name _ _ _ _ _ _ _ _ _ _ _ _ _ _ Day _ _ _ _ _ _ _ _ _

Circle or highlight the correct word.

   milk   melt   old   salt

   melt   milk   quilt   help

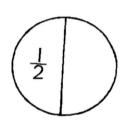   filth   shelf   help   half

   help   melt   cold   old

   old   cold   salt   filth

   help   milk   melt   salt

Name _ _ _ _ _ _ _ _ _ _ _ _ _ _ Day _ _ _ _ _ _ _ _ _

Underline or highlight the words which end with 'ld', 'lk', 'lp', 'lt', 'lf', and 'lth'.

I can help poor old ted but I cannot stop the sun that melts the cold snowman.

Half of the filth is in the bin but you can help with the rest.

Name_ _ _ _ _ _ _ _ _ _ _ _ _ _ _ _ _ _ Day _ _ _ _ _ _ _ _ _

learn it	copy then cover	write then check
hand-stand		
sand		
skunk		
plank		
ink		

Fold over

Name_ _ _ _ _ _ _ _ _ _ _ _ _ _ _ _ _ Day _ _ _ _ _ _ _ _ _

Match the words and pictures. Colour each word box a different colour and use the same crayon to join each word to the correct picture.

hand-stand

sand

skunk

plank

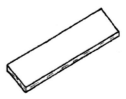

ink

Name _ _ _ _ _ _ _ _ _ _ _ _ _ _ _   Day _ _ _ _ _ _ _ _ _

Copy these words.

hand-stand	ink	skunk	plank	sand
_____	____	____	____	__

Choose the right word for each space below.

1. Blip can _ _ _ _ _ _ on his hand.

2. This _ _ _ _ _ has a bad stink.

3. I can dig in the _ _ _ _.

4. He can make a shelf with a _ _ _ _ _ _.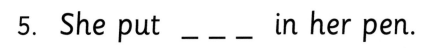

5. She put _ _ _ in her pen.

Name_ _ _ _ _ _ _ _ _ _ _ _ _ _ _ _ _ _ Day _ _ _ _ _ _ _ _ _ _

learn it	copy then cover	write then check
tent		
bent		
lunch		
branch		
bench		

Fold over

Name_ _ _ _ _ _ _ _ _ _ _ _ _ _ _ _ Day _ _ _ _ _ _ _ _ _

**Match the words and pictures. Colour each word box
a different colour and use the same crayon to join
each word to the correct picture.**

| bent |

| tent |

| lunch |

| branch |

| bench |

Name _ _ _ _ _ _ _ _ _ _ _ _ _ _ Day _ _ _ _ _ _ _ _ _

Copy these words.

branch	bench	bent	tent	lunch
___	___	___	___	___

Choose the right word for each space below.

1. We can sit on this _ _ _ _ _ .

2. Tum is in his _ _ _ _ .

3. He has _ _ _ _ _ and a drink

 with a _ _ _ _ straw.

5. The bird sat on the _ _ _ _ _ _ .

Name _ _ _ _ _ _ _ _ _ _ _ _ _ _ Day _ _ _ _ _ _ _ _ _

Circle or highlight the correct word.

   tent   lunch   branch   bench

   plank   pink   ink   skunk

   hand   stand   plank   sand

   bent   tent   bench   lunch

   branch   bench   lunch   tent

   plank   skunk   ink   bent

Name _ _ _ _ _ _ _ _ _ _ _ _ _ _ Day _ _ _ _ _ _ _ _ _

Underline or highlight the words which end with 'nd', 'nk', 'nt', and 'nch'.

Blip sat on a bench on a sand bank. He has lunch and a drink with a bent straw.

He digs in the sand. He is glad and stands on his hands.

Name_ _ _ _ _ _ _ _ _ _ _ _ _ _ Day _ _ _ _ _ _ _ _ _

learn it	copy then cover	write then check
act		
left		
gift		
lift		
swift		

Fold over

Name_ _ _ _ _ _ _ _ _ _ _ _ _ _ _ _ Day _ _ _ _ _ _ _ _ _

Match the words and pictures. Colour each word box a different colour and use the same crayon to join each word to the correct picture.

act

turn

left

gift

lift

swift

Name _ _ _ _ _ _ _ _ _ _ _ _ _ Day _ _ _ _ _ _ _ _

Copy these words.

act	left	gift	lift	swift

Choose the right word for each space below.

1. Blip can _ _ _.

2. Pot can _ _ _ _.

3. A _ _ _ _ _ _ is a fast bird.

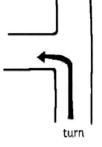

4. Here is a _ _ _ _.

5. Next, we go _ _ _ _.

turn

Name_ _ _ _ _ _ _ _ _ _ _ _ _ _ _ _ _ Day _ _ _ _ _ _ _ _ _ _

learn it	**copy then cover**	**write then check**
slept		
nest		
mast		
fist		
next		

Fold over

Name _ _ _ _ _ _ _ _ _ _ _ _ _ _ _ Day _ _ _ _ _ _ _ _ _

**Match the words and pictures. Colour each word box
a different colour and use the same crayon to join
each word to the correct picture.**

slept

nest

mast

fist

next

Name _ _ _ _ _ _ _ _ _ _ _ _ _ _ Day _ _ _ _ _ _ _ _ _ _

Copy these words.

slept	nest	mast	fist	next

Choose the right word for each space below.

1. This boat has a _ _ _ _.

2. The cat _ _ _ _ _ on the bed.

3. His hand is in a _ _ _ _.

4. Four eggs in a _ _ _ _ .

5. Put in the _ _ _ _ one.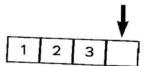

Name _ _ _ _ _ _ _ _ _ _ _ _ _ _ _ Day _ _ _ _ _ _ _ _ _

Circle or highlight the correct word.

   tact   fact   act   left

   kept   wept   slept   mast

   gift   lift   swift   left

   mast   fist   fast   nest

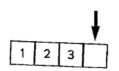   nest   next   mast   fist

   swift   lift   gift   left

Name _ _ _ _ _ _ _ _ _ _ _ _ _ _ Day _ _ _ _ _ _ _ _ _

Underline or highlight the words which end with 'ct', 'ft', 'pt', 'st' and 'xt'.

Blip went into a shop. He had to go left and then up in a lift. Next, he had to get a gift for his pal, Pot.

He got a model ship with a mast. He put it in a gift box.

Name_ _ _ _ _ _ _ _ _ _ _ _ _ _ _ _ _ Day _ _ _ _ _ _ _ _ _

learn it	copy then cover	write then check
ask		
flask		
mask		
bask		
jump		

Fold over

65

Name_ _ _ _ _ _ _ _ _ _ _ _ _ _ _ _ Day _ _ _ _ _ _ _ _ _

Match the words and pictures. Colour each word box a different colour and use the same crayon to join each word to the correct picture.

ask

flask

mask

bask

jump

Name _____ Day _____

Copy these words.

ask	flask	mask	bask	jump
_____	_____	_____	_____	_____

Choose the right word for each space below.

1. He did six _ _ _ _ s.

2. Put on this _ _ _ _.

3. He had a drink from his _ _ _ _ _.

4. Pod can _ _ _ _ in the sun.

5. Pod _ _ _ s the way to go.

Name_ _ _ _ _ _ _ _ _ _ _ _ _ _ _ Day _ _ _ _ _ _ _ _ _

learn it	copy then cover	write then check
lamp		
clamp		
stamp		
wasp		
gasp		

Fold over

Name_ _ _ _ _ _ _ _ _ _ _ _ _ _ _ _ _ Day _ _ _ _ _ _ _ _ _

Match the words and pictures. Colour each word box a different colour and use the same crayon to join each word to the correct picture.

lamp

clamp

stamp

wasp

gasp

Name _ _ _ _ _ _ _ _ _ _ _ _ _ _ Day _ _ _ _ _ _ _ _ _ _

Copy these words.

lamp	clamp	stamp	wasp	gasp
____	____	____	____	____

Choose the right word for each space below.

1. The _ _ _ _ is lit.

2.  She _ _ _ _ s with shock.

3. This _ _ _ _ can sting you.

4. Here is a _ _ _ _ _.

5. He held the plank with a _ _ _ _ _.

Name _ _ _ _ _ _ _ _ _ _ _ _ _ _ Day _ _ _ _ _ _ _ _ _

Circle or highlight the correct word.

ramp   clamp   lump   jump

flask   mask   bask   ask

clamp   ramp   lamp   jump

mask   gasp   wasp   flask

task   mask   flask   ask

Name _ _ _ _ _ _ _ _ _ _ _ _ _ _ Day _ _ _ _ _ _ _ _ _ _

Underline or highlight the words which end with 'sk', 'mp', and 'sp'.

"Can a wasp sting me?" Sal asks her mum.

"Yes, it can," said Mum. Sal gasps with

shock as she looks at a wasp on her flask.

"Jump on it and squash it" says Mum.

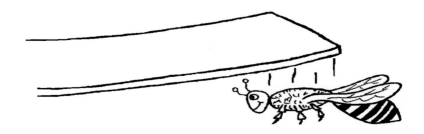